CAKES & COOKIES
FOR BEGINNERS

Fiona Watt

Designed by Mary Cartwright
Illustrated by Kim Lane
Photography by Howard Allman
Recipes by Julia Kirby-Jones
American editor: Peggy Porter Tierney

Food preparation by Ricky Turner and Lizzie Harris
Cover illustration by Christyan Fox

Contents

Before you begin

Before you start to bake, read through the tips on these pages. Each recipe has a list of ingredients that you will need. Make sure that you have them all before you begin.

In most types of cooking, it doesn't matter if you change an ingredient or leave something out, but you can't do this when you are baking. It's also important that you measure things exactly and use the right size of pan, otherwise your cakes or cookies may not turn out correctly.

Take butter or margarine out of the refrigerator at least 30 minutes before you use it, unless the recipe says something different.

Always use large-sized eggs unless the recipe says something else.

When you measure with a spoon, use a level spoonful, not a heaped one.

Equipment

If you are making a cake, use the size and shape of pan written in the recipe. If you use a different size, you may not have the correct amount of mixture

Cookie sheets

The cookies in this book are baked on cookie sheets. Space out the uncooked cookies as they usually increase in size as they cook. When you use two cookie sheets, put them into your oven one above the other. Cook the top one for the time the recipe says, then take it out. Move the bottom one up and cook until it's ready

Your oven

Turn your oven on when the recipe tells you to, so that it heats up.

Preparing cake pans

You need to grease a cake pan or cookie sheet to stop the cake or cookie mixture from sticking to it when it's cooked. To grease a pan, dip a paper towel into soft butter or margarine. Rub the towel over the bottom. In some recipes you also need to line the pan with wax paper or rice paper, or sprinkle it with flour. To flour a pan after you have greased it, add a tablespoon or two of flour.

Cooling

Make sure that you always wear oven mitts when you take anything out of the oven. Leave cakes or cookies in their pan or on the cookie sheets for several minutes to cool. Then, put them on a wire rack to cool down completely.

Grease the sides too.

Tip the pan from side to side, until there is a light dusting all over. Throw away the excess flour.

To remove a cake from a loose-bottomed cake pan, put the pan onto a can. Press on the side of the pan so that it slides down.

Which shelf?

Cook your cake or cookies on a shelf in the middle of your oven unless the recipe says something different. Always move the shelf to the middle before you turn on your oven. Don't leave an empty shelf above it.

To turn a cake out of a cake pan, put a wire rack on top of the pan. Turn it over so that the cake comes out.

Baking tips

These pages give you lots of cooking hints and tips that will help you with the recipes in this book. You'll also find other hints spread throughout the book.

Breaking an egg

1. Crack the egg sharply on the rim of a cup or bowl. Push your thumbs into the crack in the shell and pull the sides apart.

2. Before you add an egg to a mixture, break the egg into a separate cup or bowl. It helps you to pick out any shell which may fall in.

Separating eggs

Don't let the yolk break.

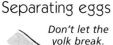

Leave the yolk on the saucer.

Egg whites will not whisk if the bowl or whisk are greasy.

1. You will need a bowl and a saucer for this. Crack the egg on the side of the bowl, then pour it slowly onto the saucer.

2. Carefully put a small cup over the yolk. Tip the saucer over the bowl so that the egg white dribbles into it.

If you are whisking the egg whites, make sure that your bowl and whisk are clean and dry before you start (see page 29).

Beating eggs

Beat with the fork like this.

Beating a mixture

If you are beating eggs, you can use a fork instead of a whisk. Beat them until the white and yolk are mixed together.

1. Before you begin to beat a mixture, put your bowl on a damp dishcloth. This stops the bowl from slipping as you beat.

2. Stir the mixture briskly with a wooden spoon or a whisk. You are trying to get the mixture as smooth and creamy as you can.

ifting

Shake the strainer until all the flour falls through.

ut a strainer over a bowl nd pour the flour into it. you sift whole-wheat lour, tip any bran left in he strainer into the bowl.

Rubbing in

1. Cut the butter or margarine into small pieces and stir it into the flour. Stir until each piece is covered with flour.

Do this with clean, dry hands.

2. Rub the pieces with your fingertips. Lift the mixture and let it fall as you rub. Do this until it becomes like fine breadcrumbs.

olling out

. Sprinkle a clean, dry vork surface with a little lour. Put the dough onto t, then sprinkle a rolling in with some flour.

2. Press the rolling pin onto the dough and roll it away from you. Turn the dough in a quarter turn and roll it again.

Shape the dough with your hands to keep it circular.

3. Continue rolling and turning to make a circle, until you get the thickness of dough written in the recipe.

Melting chocolate

. Heat about an inch of vater in a pan so that it is ubbling gently. Break he chocolate into a eatproof bowl.

Stir the chocolate as it melts.

2. Put on some oven mitts and lift the bowl into the pan. The heat from the water melts the chocolate gradually.

Testing a cake

At the end of the cooking time, test your cake to see if it is cooked. Press it in the middle. If it is cooked, it will feel firm and spring up.

Peanut butter cookies

Makes 12 cookies

4 tablespoons butter or margarine
¾ cup packed soft light brown sugar
½ cup crunchy peanut butter
½ cup self-rising flour
1 cup oatmeal
1 large egg

For the topping:
  ½ cup chopped peanuts

Grease two cookie sheets with butter or margarine. Turn the oven on to 325°F so that it can heat up.

2. Put the margarine or butter into a large bowl. Add the sugar and peanut butter. Beat them until they are light and creamy.

3. Put a strainer over the bowl and sift the flour onto the mixture. Add the oatmeal and stir well to mix everything together.

4. Press the mixture with your fingers, then fold it in half and press again. Do this again and again until it makes a soft dough.

5. Divide the mixture in half, then in quarters until you make 12 pieces. Squeeze each piece to make a small ball.

6. Put the balls onto the cookie sheets, leaving plenty of space between them. Flatten them slightly with your hand.

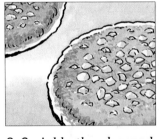

7. Break the egg into a small bowl and beat it well with a fork. Brush the top of each cookie with some beaten egg.

8. Sprinkle the chopped peanuts all over the top of each cookie. They will stick to the egg which you have brushed on.

9. Bake the cookies for 15 minutes, until they are golden. Leave them on the trays to cool a little, then lift them onto a wire rack.

Corn flake crunch

Makes 8 pieces

8oz. semi-sweet baking chocolate
3 tablespoons of maple syrup
4 tablespoons margarine
5 cups of corn flakes

an 8-inch shallow, round pan

1. Grease the pan with a little butter or margarine on paper towels. Grease the inside well, but do not use too much butter.

2. Break the chocolate into a large pan. Add the syrup and margarine. Heat the pan gently, stirring all the time.

Lift the pieces out with a blunt knife or a spatula.

3. When the chocolate has melted, add the corn flakes and stir them well. Make sure that they are coated all over with chocolate.

4. Spoon the mixture into the pan. Gently smooth the top with the back of a spoon. Try not to crush the corn flakes.

5. Put the pan in a refrigerator for the chocolate to set. It will take about two hours. Cut it into eight pieces.

Marshmallow crispies

Makes 15 pieces

4oz. wrapped toffees or slab toffee
½ cup margarine
2 cups marshmallows
7 cups puffed rice cereal
a shallow 11 x 7 inch pan

1. Grease the pan (see page 3). If you are using a slab of toffee, put it in a plastic bag and break it up with a rolling pin.

They will take about 15 minutes to melt.

2. Put the toffee, margarine and marshmallows into a large pan. Melt them very gently over a low heat, stirring all the time.

3. When everything has melted and blended together, take the pan off the heat. Gently stir in the puffed rice cereal.

4. Spoon the mixture into the pan and press it gently with the back of a metal spoon. Leave the mixture to set, then cut it up.

Chocolate chip cookies

½ cup butter or margarine
½ cup sugar
½ cup brown sugar
1 egg
half a teaspoon of vanilla extract
6oz. chocolate chips
1¼ cups flour
½ teaspoon baking soda

Makes 12

Use a wooden spoon.

1. Grease two large cookie sheets with butter or margarine (see page 3). Turn your oven on to 350°F to heat up.

2. Put the white and brown sugar and the butter or margarine into a large bowl. Beat it briskly until it is light and creamy (see page 4).

Press down on each cookie.

3. Break the egg into a small bowl and beat it well. Stir in the vanilla, then add the mixture to the large bowl.

4. Sift the flour and the baking soda into the large bowl and stir well to make a smooth mixture. Stir in 4oz. of the chocolate chips.

5. Put a heaped tablespoon of the mixture onto a cookie sheet. Use up the rest of the mixture to make eleven more cookies.

6. Flatten each cookie slightly with the back of a fork. Sprinkle the top of each one with some of the remaining chocolate chips.

7. Bake the cookies for 10-15 minutes. They should be pale golden brown and slightly soft in the middle.

8. Leave the cookies for a few minutes, then use a spatula to lift them onto a wire rack. Leave them to cool.

Hazelnut cookies

Makes 15

⅔ cup butter or margarine
½ cup brown sugar
½ teaspoon vanilla
¼ cup cocoa powder
3oz. chopped hazelnuts or pecans
½ teaspoon baking soda
1¼ cups flour
½ cup sugar
1 egg

You could press a whole nut into the middle of the cookies before you bake them.

1. Follow steps 1-3 of the chocolate chip cookies, using the quantities of ingredients, shown in the list above.

2. Sift the flour and the cocoa powder into the bowl. Use a large spoon to stir it in well, until you get a smooth mixture.

Flatten them with the back of a spoon.

3. Cut the nuts up if necessary, asking an adult for help. Add them to the mixture and stir them in.

4. Put 15 heaped teaspoonfuls of the mixture onto the cookie sheets. Space them out. Flatten each one a little.

5. Bake the cookies for 10-15 minutes. They will darken. Leave them to cool a little, then lift them onto a wire rack.

Shortbread

Makes 8 pieces

1½ cups flour
½ cup butter, refrigerated
¼ cup sugar

an 8-inch shallow pan

1. Turn your oven on to 300°F to heat up. Grease the inside of the pan with butter on a paper towel.

2. Put a strainer over a large mixing bowl and pour the flour into it. Shake the flour into the bowl.

3. Cut the butter into small pieces and put them into the bowl. Mix them with a blunt knife to coat them with flour.

4. Rub the pieces of butter between your fingertips. Lift the mixture and let it fall back into the bowl as you rub (see page 5).

5. Continue rubbing in the flour until the mixture looks like breadcrumbs. Stir in the sugar with a wooden spoon.

6. Holding the bowl in one hand, squeeze the mixture into a ball. The heat from your hand makes the mixture stick together.

Cut across it again, before lifting it out.

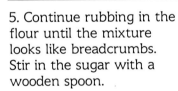

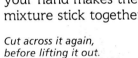

7. Press the mixture into the pan with your fingers, then use the back of a spoon to smooth the top and make it level.

8. Use the prongs of a fork to press a pattern around the edge. Then cut the mixture into eight equal pieces.

9. Bake it for 30 minutes, until it becomes golden. Leave the shortbread for five minutes before putting it on a wire rack.

Gingerbread cookies

Makes about 20 cookies

2 cups flour
2 teaspoons of ground ginger
2 teaspoons of baking soda
½ cup butter or margarine
¾ cup soft light brown sugar
¾ cup white sugar
1 egg
4 tablespoons of maple syrup

large cookie cutters

1. Dip a paper towel in some margarine and rub it over two cookie sheets. Turn on your oven to 375°F to heat up.

2. Sift the flour, ginger and baking soda into a mixing bowl. Cut the butter or margarine into chunks and add them.

3. Rub the butter or margarine into the flour with your fingers, until the mixture looks like fine breadcrumbs (see page 5).

Look at the tip for measuring syrup, below right.

4. Stir the sugar into the mixture. Break the egg into a small bowl. Add the syrup to the egg and beat them together well.

5. Stir the eggy mixture into the flour. Mix everything together with a metal spoon until it makes a dough.

6. Sprinkle a clean work surface with flour and put the dough onto it. Stretch the dough by pushing it away from you.

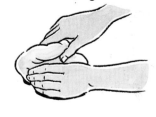

7. Fold the dough in half. Turn it and push it away from you again. Continue to push, turn and fold until the dough is smooth.

You can use any shape of cutter you like.

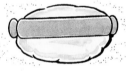

8. Cut the dough in half. Sprinkle a little more flour onto your work surface. Roll out the dough until it is about ¼in. thick.

Spread the shapes out on the cookie sheet.

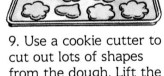

9. Use a cookie cutter to cut out lots of shapes from the dough. Lift the shapes onto the cookie sheets with a spatula.

10. Roll out the other half of dough and cut shapes from it. Squeeze the scraps of dough to make a ball. Roll it out and cut more shapes.

11. Put the cookies on the cookie sheets into your oven and bake them for 12-15 minutes. They will turn golden brown.

12. Leave the cookies on the sheets for about five minutes. Then, lift them onto a wire rack. Leave them to cool.

Measuring syrup

Heat your spoon in hot water before you measure syrup. It makes it easier for the syrup to slide off.

15

Oatmeal squares

Makes 12

¾ cup margarine
¾ cup brown sugar
2 tablespoons of corn syrup
2½ cups oatmeal

a shallow 7 x 11 inch pan

1. Put the pan on baking parchment or wax paper and draw around it. Cut out the rectangle just inside the line.

Cut the squares while they are in the pan and still warm.

Grease the pan well.

2. Grease the bottom of the cake pan and put the paper in. Grease the paper. Turn on your oven to 325°F.

3. Put the margarine in a large pan with the sugar and syrup. Melt the margarine gently. Do not allow the mixture to boil.

4. Take the pan off the heat. Add the oatmeal and stir them in really well so that they are covered in the margarine mixture.

5. Spoon the oatmeal into he pan. Spread them all over the bottom, then smooth the top with the back of a metal spoon.

6. Put the pan on the middle shelf in your oven and bake the mixture for 25 minutes until the oats turns golden brown.

7. Take the pan out of the oven and leave it for ten minutes. Cut the mixture into pieces. Leave them in the pan until they are cold.

Chocolate refrigerator cake

Makes about 12 slice[s]

4oz. semi-sweet baking chocolat[e]
Or, 4oz. white baking chocolat[e]
½ cup butter or margarin[e]
5 tablespoons of corn syru[p]
8oz. vanilla wafer cookie[s]
2 tablespoons of choppe[d]
maraschino cherrie[s]
2 tablespoons of raisin[s]
2 tablespoons of chopped nut[s]

an 8-inch round pa[n]

*Find out how to grease
a pan on page 3.*

*Use white
or plain
chocolate for
this recipe.*

1. Put your cake pan onto
wax paper and draw
around it. Cut out the
circle, just inside the line
you have drawn.

2. Grease the pan. Put in
the wax paper circle you
have cut out. Grease it
again, on top of the pape[r]
circle.

. Break the chocolate into pieces and put it in a saucepan. Add the butter or margarine and spoon in the syrup.

4. Put the pan over a low heat and let the mixture melt. Stir it occasionally. When the mixture has melted, turn off the heat.

5. Break the cookies into pieces and put them into a bowl. Crush the pieces of cookies finely with a rolling pin or kitchen mallet.

. Put the chopped berries, raisins and chopped nuts into the bowl. Add the mixture from the pan and stir well.

7. Spoon the mixture into the cake pan. Press it down really well, then smooth the top with the back of a metal spoon.

8. Put the pan into a refrigerator and leave it overnight. Turn the cake out and pull off the paper. Cut the cake into wedges.

Macaroons

Makes 12

3 large eggs (you only need the whites)
12 whole blanched almonds
⅓ cup sugar
4oz. ground almonds
⅓ cup flour
a few drops of almond extract

Grease the top of the paper.

1. Turn your oven on to 300°F. Cover the cookie sheets with either rice paper or baking parchment.

If you don't have rice paper or baking parchment, cover the cookie sheets with wax paper. Grease the paper lightly.

Be careful not to break the yolk.

You don't need the yolks.

Lift them out with a teaspoon.

2. Break the egg on the side of a bowl. Hold it over a saucer and pull the sides apart. Let the egg fall gently onto a saucer.

3. Hold a small cup over the egg yolk and tip the egg white into a large mixing bowl. Do the same with the other eggs.

4. Put the almonds into the egg white, then lift them out with a spoon. Put them on a plate and leave them on one side.

Make sure your whisk is clean and dry before you begin.

Use a metal spoon to fold the mixture (see the tip, page 47).

5. Beat the egg whites with an electric mixer or whisk until it forms small peaks (see tip, page 29).

6. Add the sugar, ground almonds, flour and almond extract. Fold the mixture over and over gently to mix them.

7. Put a heaped teaspoon of the mixture onto the paper on the cookie sheet and flatten it slightly with the back of the spoon.

...he macaroons spread
...s they cook.

You can eat any rice paper left on the bottom.

8. Use up the rest of the mixture in the same way, leaving a space between each spoonful. Press an almond onto each one.

9. Bake the macaroons for 25-30 minutes, until they are pale golden brown. Leave them on the cookie sheets for five minutes.

10. Lift the macaroons onto a wire rack to cool. If you have used rice paper, tear away the paper around each macaroon.

Jam cookies

Makes 12 cookies

1½ cups self-rising flour
½ cup butter or margarine
½ cup sugar
1 large egg
1 tablespoon of milk
strawberry jam

You don't have to use strawberry jam; you could try different flavors, such as apricot or plum.

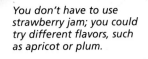

1. Turn your oven on to 400°F. Grease two cookie sheets and sprinkle them with flour. Shake them to spread the flour, then tip off the excess.

2. Put a strainer over a large bowl and shake the flour through it. Cut the butter or margarine into small chunks and add them to the flour.

3. Rub the chunks of butter or margarine into the flour with your fingers, until it looks like fine breadcrumbs (see page 5). Stir in the sugar.

4. Break the egg into a small bowl and add the milk. Whisk them together, then stir them into the mixture in the large bowl.

5. Sprinkle a clean work surface with some flour. Press the mixture together to make a firm ball, then put it onto your work surface.

Don't try to eat them while they are hot. The jam could burn you.

6. Cut the ball in half. Then, cut each half into three pieces. Cut each of the pieces in half. You should end up with 12 even-sized pieces.

7. Squeeze each piece into a round shape and spread them out on the cookie sheets. Make a dent in each cookie and fill it with a teaspoon of jam.

8. Bake the cookies for ten minutes. They will rise and turn golden. Lift each one onto a wire rack and leave them to cool before eating them.

Chocolate choux buns

Makes about 12 buns

⅔ cup cold water
1 teaspoon sugar
4 tablespoons butter
⅓ cup and 1 tablespoon flour
2 eggs

For the filling:
1 cup whipping cream

For the icing:
6oz. semi-sweet baking chocolate
¼ cup powdered sugar

1. Turn on your oven to 400°F. Dip a paper towel in some margarine and rub it over two cookie sheets.

2. Hold each cookie sheet under cold running water Shake them well to get rid of all the drops of water.

3. Put a strainer over a bowl and pour in the flour. Sift the flour into the bowl. Put this on one side. You'll need it later.

Beat the mixture quickly to mix in all the flour.

4. Put the water, sugar and butter into a large saucepan. Place the pan over a medium heat to melt the butter.

5. As soon as the butter has melted, turn up the heat and bring the mixture to a boil. Then, turn off the heat.

6. Immediately, shoot all the flour into the pan at one time, and start to beat the mixture really well with a wooden spoon.

7. Keep beating the mixture until it makes a ball of smooth paste which leaves the sides of the pan clean.

8. Break the eggs into a small bowl and beat them. Add them, a little at a time, beating the mixture each time you add some.

9. Put teaspoonfuls of the mixture onto the cookie sheets. Make sure that they are spaced out. They will spread as they cook.

Slit the buns to allow the hot air inside to escape.

10. Bake them for 25-30 minutes, until they are golden brown. Make a slit in each one and leave them on a rack to cool.

11. Beat the cream until it is stiff. Cut the buns in half. Fill them with a teaspoon of cream, then press them together again.

12. Break the chocolate into chunks and let it melt in a bowl over a saucepan of hot water (see page 5). Stir in the sugar.

13. Using a teaspoon, carefully coat the top of each bun with the melted chocolate. Leave the chocolate to harden.

Scones

Makes 16 scones

1¼ cups self-rising flour
1 level teaspoon of baking powder
a pinch of salt
4 tablespoons butter or margarine
⅛ cup sugar
2oz. raisins
½ cup milk

2½-inch cookie cutter

You can also make fruit scones by adding 2oz. of chopped maraschino cherries or chopped dates, with the sugar at step 3.

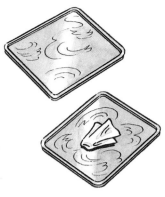

Hold the strainer up above the bowl.

1. Turn your oven on to heat up to 450°F. Grease two cookie sheets with butter or margarine on a paper towel.

2. Sift the flour, baking powder and salt into a bowl. Cut the butter or margarine into small pieces and add them to the flour.

Use your fingertips.

3. Rub the butter or margarine into the flour until the mixture looks like fine breadcrumbs. Add the sugar, raisins and milk.

4. Use a blunt knife to mix everything to make a soft dough. Then, press and mold it with your fingers until it's smooth.

5. Sprinkle an area of your work surface with flour and put the dough onto it. Roll it out until the dough is about ½ inch thick.

Cut the circles close together.

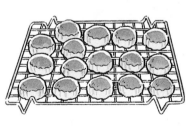

6. Cut circles from the dough with the cutter. Squeeze the scraps into a ball and roll them out again. Cut more circles.

7. Put the circles onto the cookie sheets, leaving quite a lot of space between each one. Brush the tops with a little milk.

8. Bake the scones for 7-10 minutes on the top shelf of the oven. They will rise and turn golden. Lift them onto a wire rack to cool.

Baked cheesecake squares

Makes 15 squares

1¼ cups flour
½ cup butter
1 tablespoon of sugar
2 tablespoons of water

a 7 x 11 x 1 inch pan

For the filling: 6oz. (⅔ cup) sour cream
8oz. ricotta cheese
¼ cup sugar
a lemon
3 medium eggs
½ cup raisins

Rub in the butter until it looks like breadcrumbs.

1. Draw around the pan on baking parchment or wax paper. Cut out the shape. Grease the pan and put the paper into it.

2. Turn your oven on to 400°F. Sift the flour. Cut the butter into small pieces and rub it in (see page 5).

3. Stir in the sugar. Add the water and mix to make a soft dough. Mix it until the mixture leaves the side of the bowl clean.

Beat the mixture until smooth.

4. Put the dough into the pan and press it with your fingers to cover the bottom of the pan. Press it right into the corners.

5. Prick the dough all over with a fork. Bake it for 10 minutes until it is golden brown. Turn the oven down to 325°F.

6. Put the sour cream, cheese and sugar into a bowl. Grate the yellow rind off the lemon and add it. Beat the mixture well.

Turn the mixture over and over.

7. Separate the eggs (see page 4). Put the whites into a medium-sized bowl. Add the yolks to the mixture and beat it again.

8. Beat the egg whites until they are stiff (see right). Fold them gently into the mixture with a metal spoon (see page 39).

9. Sprinkle the raisins over the dough and pour the eggy mixture on top. Bake for 45-50 minutes until it is golden brown.

Whisking egg whites

1. Separate the egg whites from their yolks and put them into a clean, dry bowl. Make sure that no yolk gets into the bowl.

2. Hold the bowl tightly in one hand and twist the whisk around and around. The egg will begin to become white and frothy.

3. Continue whisking until the whites get stiff and you get points or 'peaks' forming on the top when you lift up the whisk.

Chocolate brownies

Makes 15

¾ cup margarine
1⅔ cup sugar
1 teaspoon of vanilla extract
3 eggs
1 cup flour
1 level teaspoon of baking powder
1 cup cocoa
6oz. walnuts or pecan nuts

a rectangular pan, 9 x 12 inch

Use wax paper or baking parchment.

1. You will need to grease and flour, or grease and line your pan. If lining, draw around the pan on the paper and cut it out.

2. If you have lined the pan, grease it, then lay the paper in the pan and grease the top of it. Turn the oven on to 350°F.

3. Put the margarine into a pan and melt it over a low heat. Pour it into a large mixing bowl, then add the sugar and vanilla extract.

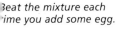

Beat the mixture each time you add some egg.

4. Break the eggs into a small bowl and beat them. Add them to the large bowl, a little at a time. Beat them in well.

5. Sift the flour into the bowl and add the baking powder and the cocoa. Stir everything together so that it is mixed well.

6. Cut the nuts up, keeping your fingers away from the blade. Add them to the mixture and stir it well again.

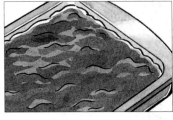

7. Pour the mixture into the cake pan and smooth the top with the back of a spoon. Bake it for about 40 minutes.

8. The brownies are ready when they have risen and have formed a crust on top. They should still be soft in the middle.

Use a spatula to lift them.

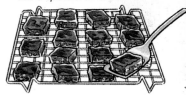

9. Leave the brownies in the pan for five minutes, then cut them into 15 squares. Leave them on a wire rack to cool.

Pecan squares

Makes 12 squares

For the base: ¾ cup butter or margarine
¾ cup powdered sugar
1¼ cups flour

For the topping: ⅓ cup butter or margarine
2 tablespoons of maple syrup
2 tablespoons of milk
1 teaspoon of vanilla extract
½ cup soft brown sugar
2 eggs
4oz. pecan nuts

a 7 x 11 inch pan

Put the pan onto a piece of wax paper or baking parchment. Draw round it and cut out the shape you have drawn.

2. Grease the pan. Put the paper into the bottom of the pan and press it down. Turn the oven on to 350°F.

3. For the base, put the butter or margarine into a mixing bowl. Add the sugar and beat it until it is light and creamy.

4. Sift the flour into the bowl and stir it in well. Sprinkle flour onto a clean work surface and put the mixture onto it.

5. Press the mixture with your fingers, fold it in half, then press again. Do this again and again for about a minute.

6. Use the back of a spoon to press the mixture over the bottom of the pan. Bake it for about 15 minutes or until it is golden brown.

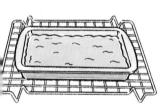

7. When the base has cooked, leave it in the pan, but put it on a wire rack to cool. Begin to make the topping while it cools.

8. Put the butter or margarine into a pan and melt it over a low heat. Stir in the syrup, sugar, milk and vanilla.

9. Break the eggs into a small bowl and beat them well. Take the pan off the heat and stir the beaten eggs into the mixture.

10. Pour the topping onto the base. Sprinkle the pecan nuts evenly over the topping and bake it for about 25 minutes.

11. The topping will turn dark golden brown, but it should be slightly gooey in the middle. Leave it to cool in the pan.

12. When it has cooled, cut it into 12 squares, by making two cuts lengthwise along the pan, then three cuts across.

Banana and nut cake

Makes 9 slice[s]

½ cup butter or margarin[e]
1 cup light brown sug[ar]
2 egg[s]
2 banana[s]
⅔ cup self-rising flou[r]
1 teaspoon of baking powde[r]
4oz. chopped nu[ts]

an 8-inch square cake pa[n]

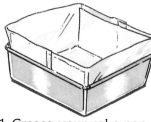

1. Grease your cake pan with butter or margarine on a paper towel. Flour it or line it with paper as or page 35.

2. Turn on your oven to 375°F to heat up. Put the butter or margarine into [a] mixing bowl. Add the sugar.

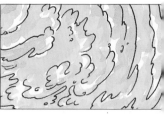

3. Use a wooden spoon to beat the butter or margarine and the sugar, until they are very smooth and creamy.

. Carefully break the
ggs into a small bowl.
eat them with a whisk
r a fork until they are
nixed well (see page 4).

5. Add the beaten egg to
the creamy mixture, a
little at a time. Each time
you add some egg, beat it
into the mixture.

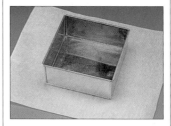

Greasing & lining a pan

Put the pan on a piece of
baking parchment or
wax paper which is
larger than the pan.

. Peel the bananas. Put
hem into a bowl. Mash
hem well with the back
of a fork.

7. Stir the mashed banana
into the creamy mixture.
Put a strainer over the
bowl and sift the flour
and baking powder into it.

Use a pencil to draw
around the pan, as close
to the bottom as you
can. Lift the pan off.

. Use a metal spoon to
tir the flour into the
nixture. Do this by
urning the mixture over
lowly with the spoon.

9. Spoon the mixture into
your cake pan. Sprinkle
the top with the chopped
nuts and bake it for about
20-25 minutes.

Cut in from the edge to
each corner of the
square. Fold in each side
along its pencil line.

. Press lightly on the
op of the cake to test it.
. should spring back up.
eave it to cool in the pan
or five minutes.

11. Lift the cake out by the
paper, or turn a floured
pan upside down over a
wire rack. Leave it to cool,
then cut it into slices.

Grease the pan. Fit the
paper into the pan. Trim
off any extra paper, just
above the pan.

Simple sponge cakes

Makes 18 squares. Frost the cakes with sugar icing or butter cream frosting.

For the squares: 2 cups self-rising flour
1 cup soft margarine
4 tablespoons of milk
1 level teaspoon of baking powder
1 cup sugar
2-3 drops of vanilla extract
4 eggs

For sugar icing: 1½ cups powdered sugar
about 2 tablespoons of water

For butter cream frosting: ⅔ cup butter, softened
2½ cups powdered sugar
1 teaspoon of vanilla extract

For decorating: candy
a 13 x 9 baking pan

Find out about greasing on page 3.

Use a wooden spoon.

1. Grease the pan. Draw around it on baking parchment or wax paper. Cut out the shape and put it in the pan.

2. Turn the oven on to 350°F to heat up. Put a strainer over a large mixing bowl and sift the flour through it.

3. Add the margarine, mil baking powder, sugar and vanilla. Break the eggs into small bowl, then add ther too. Beat everything well.

Leave the cake in the pan to cool.

4. Scrape the mixture into the pan and smooth the top. Bake it for 40-45 minutes, until the cake springs up when you press the middle.

5. Make the frosting when the cake has cooled. For sugar icing: sift the powdered sugar into a bowl. Add a little water and stir.

Add some more water and stir it again. Continue to do this until the icing coats the back of the spoon and dribbles off it.

For butter cream frosting: beat the butter in a bowl until it is creamy. Sift in the powdered sugar. Add the vanilla and mix it well.

6. Lift the cake out of the pan. Spread the frosting over it. Cut the cake into squares. Decorate them before the frosting sets.

Variations

Cherry and coconut: add
6oz. chopped maraschino
cherries and 3oz. shredded
coconut to the mixture at
step 3.

Chocolate: add 2 tablespoons
of cocoa powder to the
mixture at step 3. Leave
out the vanilla extract.

Lemon: grate the rind off
two lemons and add it to
the mixture at step 3. Leave
out the vanilla extract.

Marble cake

Makes about 8 slices

1 cup butter or margarine
1⅓ cup sugar
4 eggs
1⅓ cups self-rising flour

1 teaspoon vanilla extract
an orange
2 tablespoons of cocoa powder

an 8 x 5 inch loaf pan

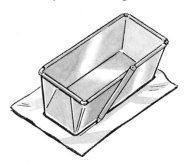

1. You will need to grease and flour or grease and line the pan. If lining, draw around the pan and cut out the shape.

2. Grease inside the pan, then flour it or put your paper in the bottom. Turn the oven on to 350°F to heat up.

3. Put the butter or margarine, vanilla and the sugar into a mixing bowl. Beat them until they are mixed well and creamy.

Beat well each time you add some egg.

4. Break the eggs into a small bowl and beat them. Add the beaten egg, a little at a time, to the creamy mixture.

5. Sift the flour into the bowl, then 'fold' it in with a metal spoon (see tip, right). Divide the mixture between two bowls.

Use the medium holes on your grater.

6. Grate the yellow rind off the orange. Be careful not to grate any of the white part under the skin as it tastes bitter.

7. Add the orange rind to one bowl and the cocoa powder to the other. Stir each bowl well, using separate spoons.

8. Put alternate spoonfuls of the mixture into the pan. Use a knife to make swirly patterns through the mixture. Smooth the top.

9. Bake the cake for an hour to an hour and 20 minutes. The cake should be well-risen and firm when you press it.

You'll see the marble effect when you cut the cake.

Folding in

10. Leave the cake in the pan for 10 minutes to cool, then turn it onto a wire rack. When it is cold, cut it into slices.

Use a metal spoon to cut through the middle of the mixture, then fold it over very gently. Do this again and again.

Continue cutting and folding until the ingredients are mixed. Folding in keeps your mixture very light.

Layered lemon cake

Makes about 12 slices

a lemon
1¾ cups self-rising flour
1 teaspoon of baking powder
3 eggs
¾ cup soft margarine
¾ cup sugar

For the filling:
2 eggs
½ cup sugar

a lemon
4 tablespoons unsalted butter

For the icing:
a lemon
1 cup powdered sugar

two round 7-inch pans

Heat your oven to 350°F.

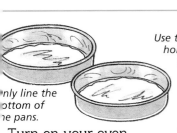
Only line the bottom of the pans.

Use the medium holes on the grater.

1. Turn on your oven. Grease and flour your pans or grease and line your pans with baking parchment or wax paper.

2. Grate the rind off a lemon, then cut the lemon in half. Twist each half on a lemon squeezer to get the juice from it.

3. Sift the flour and baking powder into a bowl. Break the eggs into a cup, then add them, along with the margarine and sugar.

Smooth the top with a spoon.

4. Beat everything in the bowl well, then stir in the lemon rind and juice. Divide the mixture between the two pans.

5. Bake the cakes for 25 minutes until they spring up when you press them in the middle. Leave them on a rack to cool.

6. While the cakes are cooling, make the filling. Break the eggs into a heatproof bowl and add the sugar.

Wear oven mitts.

It will take about 20 minutes.

7. Add the grated rind and juice of another lemon. Cut the butter into small pieces and add it to the bowl.

8. Put some water into a pan and turn on the heat so that the water is just bubbling. Put the bowl into the pan.

9. Stir the mixture from time to time as it thickens. Take it off the heat when it coats the back of your spoon. Leave it to cool.

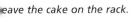
Leave the cake on the rack.

A zester gives you long pieces of rind.

Press hard as you scrape.

Stir in the juice a little at a time.

10. Spread one cake with the filling. Put the other cake carefully on top. Don't worry if some of the filling oozes out.

11. Either grate some rind from the last lemon or scrape some off with a zester, if you have one. Keep it on one side.

12. Squeeze one half of the lemon. Sift the powdered sugar. Stir in the juice until the icing is like glue. Ice the cake. Sprinkle rind on top.

Apple cake

Makes about 12 slices

1⅓ cups whole-wheat flour
1 cup sugar
1 teaspoon of baking powder
3 eggs
¾ cup soft margarine

1 rounded teaspoon of ground cinnamon
2oz. chopped nuts
1 cooking apple, approx. 8oz.
brown sugar for sprinkling on top

an 8-inch round, loose-bottomed
    cake pan

1. You will need to grease and flour or grease and line your pan. If lining, draw around the pan on the paper and cut out the circle.

2. Grease the pan, then flour it or put the paper circle in the bottom. Turn your oven on to 325°F to heat up.

3. Sift the flour into a large bowl and tip in the grainy pieces left in the bottom of your strainer. Add the sugar and baking powder.

This cake is delicious if you eat it while it is still slightly warm.

4. Break the eggs into a small bowl, then add them to the bowl along with the margarine, cinnamon and half of the nuts.

5. Use a wooden spoon to mix everything together really well. Spoon the mixture into the pan and smooth the top.

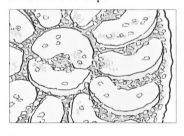

6. Peel the apple (see tip), then cut out the core. Cut the apple into thin slices. Lay the slices in circles on top, overlapping each one.

7. Sprinkle the apples with the remaining nuts and a tablespoon of brown sugar. Bake the cake for an hour, until it is firm.

Peeling apples

Put it on a wire rack to cool.

8. Leave the cake in the pan for ten minutes, before slipping off the ring of the pan and lifting the cake off the base. Leave it to cool.

Hold the apple in one hand. Scrape a potato peeler away from you again and again to remove the skin.

Apricot and orange loaf

Makes about 8 slices

4oz. (approx. 1 cup) ready-to-eat dried apricots
an orange
²⁄₃ cup self-rising flour
½ cup soft margarine
²⁄₃ cup light soft brown sugar
⅓ cup sugar
2 eggs

For the icing:
1 cup powdered sugar
2 tablespoons of orange juice

an 8 x 5 inch loaf pan

Line the pan with wax paper or baking parchment.

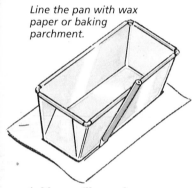

1. You will need to grease and flour or grease and line your pan. If lining, draw around your pan and cut out the shape.

2. Grease your pan and flour it, or grease it and add the paper. Turn your oven on to heat up to 350°F.

3. Use kitchen scissors to snip the dried apricots into small pieces. Cut them so that they fall into a large mixing bowl.

Use the medium holes on your grater.

Tilt the bowl slightly as you beat.

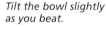

4. Grate the rind off the orange. Try not to grate any of the white pith underneath. Scrape the rind into the bowl.

5. Sift the flour into the bowl. Add the margarine and brown sugar. Break the eggs into a cup, then pour them in too.

6. Put the bowl onto a damp dishcloth. Beat the mixture firmly with a wooden spoon, until it is light and fluffy.

7. Scrape the mixture out of the bowl into the loaf pan. Smooth the top with the back of a spoon to make it level.

8. Bake the loaf for about 40 minutes, until it rises and turns golden. Leave it for a few minutes, then turn it onto a wire rack.

Pour on the icing when the loaf is cool.

9. Sift the powdered sugar into a bowl. Mix in some orange juice, a little at a time, until it is like runny glue. Pour it over the loaf.

Chocolate cobweb cake

Makes about 10 slice

2 rounded tablespoons of coco
4 tablespoons of hot wate
1 cup soft margarin
1 cup suga
4 egg
1¾ cups self-rising flou
1 level teaspoon o
baking powde

For the frostinc
8oz. semi-sweet bakin
chocolate
½ cup butte
2oz. white chocolate

two 8-inch
round pan:

*To make a differen
pattern, do straight line
across the cake and the
spread them with
skewe*

Make sure that the circles lie flat.

1. You will need to grease and flour, or grease and line your pans. If lining, put a circle of paper in the bottom of each pan.

2. Turn your oven on to 350°F. Put the cocoa into a small bowl. Add the hot water and mix until it's smooth.

3. Put the margarine, sugar, eggs, flour and baking powder into a large bowl. Beat well, then stir in the cocoa mixture.

Smooth the top with a spoon.

4. Put half the mixture into each pan. Bake the cakes for 25 minutes until they rise. Turn them out onto a wire rack to cool.

5. For the frosting, melt the plain chocolate in a bowl over a pan of hot water (see page 5). Cut up the butter and mix it in.

Cover the top and the sides.

6. Turn one cake flat-side up and spread on half of the frosting. Put the other cake on top. Spread on the rest of the frosting.

7. Break the white chocolate into pieces and put it in a heatproof bowl. Melt it over a pan of hot water. Stir as it melts.

Get someone to help you spoon in the chocolate.

8. Leave the chocolate for five minutes, then take two small plastic bags and put one inside the other. Spoon in the chocolate.

9. Hold the bag over a plate and snip off a tiny corner. Be careful or the chocolate will start to run out immediately.

Tilt the bag between each circle to stop the chocolate from running out.

10. Gently squeeze the bag as you draw a circle in the middle of the cake. Add more circles around it.

11. Drag a skewer or the tip of a knife from the center out to the edge. Do this several times to make a cobweb pattern.

Index

With thanks to Jeanne and Tom Gilbert for their help with the American edition.